The Baby Sleep System

Proven, practical advice to help you get your child to sleep

by Wendy Dean

Baby Sleep Answers Ltd

The Baby Sleep System

ISBN: 978-0-9558154-1-6

This second edition published by Baby Sleep Answers Ltd 2008
Copyright © Wendy Dean, 2006, 2008

babysleepanswers.co.uk

Designed and typeset by Whoosh Design Graphics Ltd

The Baby Sleep System

This book is dedicated to my four great children
without whom I would not have had the inspiration.

About the Author

My name is Wendy Dean and I am the mother of Ben, Caitlin and twins, Ewan and Joseph.

When my first child was born I was knocked completely sideways. I had always felt in control of my life and was very used to doing my own thing and not having to answer to anybody else. On the 26th November 1999, I found myself holding a screaming 7lb 13oz bundle and I did not know what I was supposed to do with it.

The next few months were horrible, my son refused to sleep for longer than 20 minutes during the day and woke four or five times in the night. I was afraid to ask for support from my Health Visitor and none was offered. I thought I was a bad mother who had done something wrong.

Finally, in desperation, I purchased a series of books to help us all get some sleep. Six weeks later my son, Ben, was sleeping through the night and having regular naps in the day. I resolved never to go through that experience again.

Since then I have had three more children and have written and updated The Baby Sleep System. The book is based on the best sleep advice available from dozens of books and medical journals. It has also been informed by my own personal experience and that of thousands of families who have used The Baby Sleep System and the online support forum over the years.

Go on and read the book and I guarantee that a great night's sleep will be yours.

Good luck,

Wendy Dean

The Baby Sleep System is a great book full of common sense advice for parents of babies who won't sleep though the night. Combined with the online support, it offers a lifeline to desperate parents.

I wish this book had been available 30 years ago when we started our family, as we had years of baby sleep problems with our children!

Dr Chris Steele, ITV This Morning's Resident GP

I feel like a new woman this morning and it's down to you, so a big thank-you.

Hilary, West Yorkshire

Thanks once again for your help. During the last 2 nights Lily slept from 7.30pm to 7.00 in the morning without waking up once. Hopefully that odd period is gone now and she will be fine again. Your little book is very helpful and your tips are ever so needed. Thanks once again for your kind help from all my family.

Miriam, Northampton

Just wanted to say thanks to everyone on the forum as I feel like I have a real support network here. It's motivating and inspirational to hear what people are starting to achieve and helps me through the darkest moments of my post-natal depression.

Thanks Wendy for setting this up, I don't know what I would have done if I hadn't come across you.

Ann, Oslo, Norway

Thanks so much for all your help. I really think I would have cracked up by now if it wasn't for your system!

Claire, Chorley, Lancashire

I think that your sleep system is the most amazing thing ever! I will be recommending it to anyone who will listen to me!

Kerry, Leeds, West Yorkshire

Thank you so much for all your excellent advice. The book and your back up system really make you feel like you can do it! I will definitely recommend this book to my friends.

Louisa, Cambridge

Table of Contents

1 Introduction: If I Can, You Can!

1.1 Welcome

For the past twenty years I have been lucky enough to have had a great life. I had a happy childhood, a successful school life, a fantastic career as an academic, policy maker and lecturer and I married a marvellous man.

However, in 1999 my cosy existence was turned upside down with the arrival of my first son, Ben. I had an unpleasant pregnancy, a terrible labour and suddenly found myself holding a tiny baby that screamed a lot.

For the first three weeks my darling bundle of joy seemed to be awake and crying 24 hours a day and I was physically and emotionally exhausted. During this time I had signed up to the top 4 myths about baby sleep as identified by the Millpond Children's Sleep Clinic (2005):

1. Sleep problems in babies and young children are inevitable.
2. Sleep problems are difficult to solve.
3. Children will eventually grow out of sleep problems.
4. You must grit your teeth and put up with continuous night time waking.

I gathered the little strength I had left, thought this can't be right and with a befuddled brain started to research what I could do about my dire situation.

The first book I read appeared to have been written by Mother Earth incarnate. Her solution was to strap the baby to your front and devote yourself to it entirely. That's fine if you need nothing else to satisfy you in life and have a team of staff to cook, clean, wash, iron, shop and do everything else that needs to be done in a family home. There was no way that I could physically do what this woman required of me.

I guiltily searched for another book and found an example of the second baby care genre – 'let your baby dictate to you'. By now I had been trying this for six weeks. My baby was indeed telling me what he wanted to do – sleep all day (permanently attached to my breast) and play all night. In fact he was all in favour of the Mother Earth approach outlined previously. This was not the routine that I wanted, so again I looked for another baby sleep guru.

Eventually after reading about twenty baby behaviour and care books (it's easy to do this with a baby permanently attached to your boobs making it impossible to do anything else!) there seemed to be no one perfect solution.

What was needed was a system that 'fitted' with my needs and personal set of circumstances. By being systematic I was able to work out what sleep my son and I were getting, why there wasn't enough of it and what action I could take to address the issues. By going through the process that is set out in the remainder of the book, I came up with my own system and set about trialling it on my small son.

Within two weeks he was sleeping through the night and was a delight to be with during the day. In addition, I was getting all of my housework done, we were eating something other than ready meals and I was spending time with my husband, friends and family. Believe me this was a miraculous turn around.

Since that time I have helped thousands of families who have suffered as I have. The Dream Team and I have helped them work through their child's issues and with this support they have come out of the other side.

1.2   The System

Sleep problems can be very complex in nature. The tricky bit is getting to grips with the root of the problem and then treating it with one of the effective techniques that are available. I have not invented these techniques, but they have been researched and used by many professionals around the world. The aim of this book is to help you plan a strategy to get more sleep, but one that fits with the needs of you and your child.

The success of The Baby Sleep System relies on two things; being able to implement a behaviour management strategy and developing and sticking to your own routine. It can be a very emotional and difficult process to tackle a child's sleep problem which is why help and advice is also available online through the forum at: www.babysleepanswers.co.uk.

1.3   Overview of the Book

Chapter 2 will look in more detail at baby sleep patterns, why problematic sleep patterns can happen and help you to determine if your child does indeed have a sleep problem.

Chapter 3 will outline the importance of routine and help you to put together a routine that fits with your family ethos and commitments.

Chapter 4 will provide a number of examples of routines, designed for different aged children. These are not intended to be prescriptive and can be adapted to fit around individual family dynamics.

Chapter 5 examines the importance of naps during the day and how these can be incorporated into a routine.

Chapter 6 looks at the specific issue of night feeds and how to lengthen the gap between feeds though the night.

Chapter 7 provides options for managing naps, bedtimes and night time waking. It is up to you to choose the approach that best suits you and your child.

Chapter 8 sets out how to handle specific sleep issues around settling your baby into bed, night time and early waking. There are specific sections for different aged children.

Chapter 9 looks at how to manage siblings when implementing The Baby Sleep System.

There is additional help and advice in Chapter 10 for parents of twins and multiples.

Chapter 11 summarises the key advice referred to throughout the book with 14 top tips.

Chapter 12 gives details of how to access extra support via the online forum and your Health Visitor.

The final section of The Baby Sleep System takes the form of a Workbook which allows you to design your own routine and plot your progress. Additional workbook pages can be downloaded from the Baby Sleep Answers website.

The book also has case studies at the end of key sections demonstrating how "real" families have used the Baby Sleep System to solve their baby's sleep problems.

2   Does My Child Have a Sleep Problem?

2.1   The Importance of Sleep

Sleep is an absolutely vital part of your child's development. The sleeping brain is not a resting brain. It takes the time to interpret what it has seen during the day. In addition, during the cycle of sleep extra blood is pumped to the brain resulting in enhanced alertness, better information retention and sharpened senses. The body also benefits as more blood is directed to developing muscles, tissue is repaired and white blood cells are produced, which support the immune system. Your baby needs to sleep and you as a parent can help him to develop healthy sleep patterns.

2.2   Can the Baby Sleep System Help Me?

The Baby Sleep System can help you see dramatic improvements in your child's sleep if:

Your baby or toddler's sleep pattern looks markedly different from that set out in section 2.3, i.e. not enough naps, too much sleep during the day, or too little sleep at night.

Your baby or toddler cries when you put him to bed and keeps it up for longer than 15 minutes.

Your child wakes regularly in the night, cries or shouts and doesn't go back to sleep on his own.

Your child wakes for a night feed and is over 6 months old. Many babies up to the age of 6 months still need a feed in the night. However, after this age it is no longer biologically necessary for their growth and development for them to have milk in the night. By this stage baby's nutritional needs should be met by a balanced solid diet and milk feeds taken through the day.

The remainder of the book will help you to develop a system that will address all of the above problems. Your system will be based on a solid routine of food, activity, the use of naps and a behaviour management technique. Read on to start your strategy.

2.3   What is Normal Sleep?

How much sleep do babies and toddlers need? The table below gives some average sleep times.

Age	Night-time Sleep	Daytime Sleep	No. of Naps	Total Sleep
Newborn 1 - 3 months	10	6	4 - 5	16 Hours*
3 - 6 months	10	4 - 5	3 - 4	15 Hours
6 - 18 months	11	2¼	1 - 2	13¼ Hours
18 months - 3 years	11	1¼	1	12¼ Hours
3 years+	10½	0 - 1½	0 - 1	10½ - 12 Hours

* Note: Very small babies will only sleep for 2-4 hours at a time

Remember these times are averages. Some children will sleep more, some will sleep less.

babysleepanswers.co.uk

2.4 Why Does My Baby Not Sleep Well?

There is very little easily accessible scientific evidence that explains why some babies seem to sleep well and others are poor sleepers from day one. My experience with my own children, in-depth discussions with Health Visitors, the work with my clients and my extensive research has led me to divide the causes of poor sleep into 6 categories.

2.4.1 Traumatic Birth Experience

Babies who experience a long labour and/or were dragged into the world via forceps or a ventouse are usually unsettled for the first few days following the delivery. They tend to cry more and sleep less than babies born without drama. Mothers who experience a difficult delivery are usually tired, traumatised and sometimes in severe pain after the ordeal and if not appropriately counselled can find it harder to cope in the following weeks. This combination can lead to longer term sleep problems such as those outlined below.

2.4.2 Accidental Parenting

This term was originally coined by the late Tracy Hogg (*The Baby Whisperer*, see further reading section). Babies come to rely on a "prop" to help them get to sleep. Do you routinely hold, rock, walk or bounce your baby to sleep? If the answer is yes to any of these, then you have introduced a prop. Chapter 8 will look at how you can break the habit cycle.

2.4.3 Attachment Theory Issues

Attachment theory is an area of developmental psychology that looks at how babies bond with their main carer over a period of time.

Attachment theory has become the dominant theory used today in the study of infant and toddler behaviour. The theory is too complex to look at in any great detail here, but it impacts on sleep when:

- Parents are inconsistent in the way that they respond to their baby and so he becomes preoccupied with (usually) the mother's availability.
- Baby does not feel secure when away from their main carer.
- Parents have not helped the baby to learn how to regulate stressful situations and cope with changes.

The strategies outlined in Chapter 7 all have elements intended to address attachment issues for the baby and his parents.

2.4.4 Development Milestones

Many of my clients seek help when their baby starts to wake in the night when previously they had been good sleepers. There can be a number of reasons why this occurs, but it often happens when a baby learns a new skill e.g. rolling over, sitting, crawling, standing and walking. Good sleep patterns need to be re-established before night waking becomes the norm.

2.4.5 Family Anxiety

A dramatic change in the family dynamic or established routine can disrupt sleep patterns. For example, if the main carer feels very stressed, this is transmitted to the child and she becomes unsettled. Mum returning to work often coincides with the beginnings of night time waking. Family breakdown can also affect the sleep patterns of older children.

2.4.6 Minor Illness

If a child has been ill, this can disrupt sleep patterns in the period immediately following. This is usually short lived but can become longer term if the response of the parents to the illness causes baby to form an association (see Chapter 8).

The remainder of the book will give practical advice on how you as a parent can help your baby to establish, or re-establish, healthy sleep patterns whilst maintaining a trusting and loving bond.

13

3   Routine, Routine, Routine!

The cornerstone of any strategy to teach a baby to sleep through the night is routine. Your baby or child must have a consistent day time routine that includes naps (unless the child is aged over or around 2? and no longer needs to sleep during the day), activity and sufficient food. Before you even attempt to deal with putting your child to bed or coping when he wakes in the night, you need to devise and follow a daily ritual. This is a simple concept and I am sure one that you have heard many times before. However, one routine that fits all children simply does not exist. Each family has their very own lifestyle and commitments that a baby routine has to fit around. This chapter will take you through the points that you need to consider when planning your routine.

THE POINTS MADE ARE FOR GUIDANCE ONLY

**YOU NEED TO DEVISE A ROUTINE THAT FITS WITH
YOUR FAMILY PATTERNS – USE THE ROUTINE PLANNER
IN THE WORKBOOK TO DO THIS**

3.1   Wake Up Time

What time do you want to get up? The answer to this may be 10:00am, however until your children have left home and gone off to University you might as well forget it! However, it is not unrealistic to set a time that is comfortable to the rest of the population i.e. not 4:00am. Anytime from

6:00am is deemed to be in the "normal" range. If your child currently gets up anytime from 5:00am - 6:00am, aim to have 6:00am as your waking time to begin with. If your baby does not have a regular time when he wakes, then set one based on the following considerations:

- Some people prefer to shower and eat before their baby gets up. Others are happy to leave this until later.
- Breakfast will need more time if there are children to feed who are going to school or nursery and if your baby is weaned.
- If you have children to get to school, work, or have to give your husband a lift to the station then you will have less flexibility than someone who does not.

Now you have thought this through, record your baby's get-up time in the routine planner in the work book.

3.2   Daytime Feeds

As a general rule of thumb, babies benefit from having their feeds spaced at regular intervals, and the length of these intervals depends on age. Babies fed in this way tend to be more settled because they learn that they will be fed when they are hungry and therefore do not need to snack. They will also take more food at each sitting and if they are breastfed will take the correct amount of foremilk and hind milk.

Here are the suggested feeding times for different aged children. Of course, if you have a very small or very large baby, the timings will need to be adjusted.

0 - 6 weeks: Milk should be given on a two hourly feeding cycle. Baby should have the next feed, two hours after finishing the last

throughout the day (see section 6 for the details of what to do in the evening and at night). Bottle fed babies may stretch to two and a half hours, or even three.

6 weeks – 16 weeks: Milk feeds can now be increased to three hourly intervals. If your baby is breast fed every two hours currently, then move to two and a half hours for three days and then to the full three hours. This will give your supply time to adjust to the change.

16 weeks – 4 to 6 months: Milk feeds should be moved to 4 hourly intervals. If your baby is above average weight, solids can be introduced from this point. Do not introduce cheese, yoghurt, eggs, meat or products containing gluten until she is six months old. Nuts and cow's milk should not be given until she is twelve months old. Taking these precautions will ensure that your baby minimises the risk of developing an allergy. Baby rice mixed with baby's usual milk, homemade fruit and vegetable purees and jars that say they are suitable from four months of age are fine.

Plan your milk feeds so that they happen in between the solid meals rather than giving them at the same time. The best timeslots for meals are at conventional breakfast, lunch and tea times i.e. 8am, 12pm and 4:30pm.

6 months+: Your baby can now have three full meals a day (main and dessert). This is the point where you can introduce yoghurt, cheese and cow's milk in mashed potato etc. Chicken and red meat can also be given now. The main milk feeds should still be breast milk or formula. Between now and around eight months old, he will drop the mid-morning milk feed, but will still enjoy the milk when he wakes up, in the mid-afternoon and at bedtime (see section 6 for guidance on night feeds for this age group). Again meals are best served at conventional times and if you and the rest of the family eat with him, it encourages him to eat more.

12 months+: You can now introduce cow's milk instead of breast or formula milk. If your baby is eating a full and varied diet then there is no need to purchase expensive follow-on milk. The feeding routine remains the same as for the 6 months+ baby.

Establish which feeding intervals are appropriate for the age of your child and then plot them in your routine planner in the work book. Remember to adjust the times around your own commitments i.e. school pick-ups, work, swimming classes etc. You can, of course, still feed when you are out and about. You just need to get organised! If you go out to work, ask your childcare provider to do the feeds according to the routine that you have planned. If this is not possible, then use the routine that they are using on the days when you are at home with your baby.

At this stage you will not be able to complete the timings for your night feeds on your Routine Planner. These will be covered in chapter 6.

3.3   Daytime Naps

Described below are the average number and length of naps that babies and young children need to take in order to follow a good sleep pattern. Remember all children are different so the figures should not be taken literally, they are for guidance.

0 - 3 months: Small babies tend to nap every two to three hours. The sleep cycle follows the food cycle i.e. when they are full, they sleep.

3 - 6 months: The time between naps start to lengthen to three to four hourly intervals.

6 - 9 months: Your baby will usually, by now, be taking a nap in the morning, a longer nap around lunchtime and a short nap in the afternoon. The total amount of time he will be sleeping during the day should be around three hours.

9 - 12 months: Your baby will now take a maximum of two naps, one in the morning and a longer nap after lunch.

12 months – 2 years: One two hour nap a day will be sufficient, which is best taken just after lunch. If your little one is struggling to stay awake, bring his lunchtime forward.

2 - 3 years: This is the time when many children start to drop sleep during the day altogether. They will need no longer than an hour and any nap should not be taken too close to bedtime (after 3:30pm for this age group).

Choose from the list above, the appropriate napping times for your child and write them into your routine planner in the workbook. You can always tweak them later, once you have started to implement your schedule. It is very important if you can manage it, that one nap per day is taken in her cot or a bed at the childminder's/nursery. This will stand you in good stead for sorting out night time problems. Of course if you work, you will have less control over when your baby is put down for a nap. You should discuss this with your nursery or childminder to see if they would be willing to try and stick to the same regular times. If they have a policy of putting all children down for a sleep together, note that time and put her down at home then as well.

3.4 Fitting Activity around Home and Work Commitments

No matter what your personal circumstances, your baby needs some activity and a change of scenery as a part of his day. If your child attends nursery or other formal childcare setting, an activity programme will already be in place. If you are a full or part time "stay at home" mum it is important that you get out of the house at some point. The best time to do this is in the morning for two reasons:

- The many activities that are available for mums and babies tend to happen in the morning. There is a huge choice from baby music classes to gymnastics, to mother and toddler groups to activities run by charitable organisations there to support families e.g. National Childbirth Trust Coffee Mornings. Of course you do not have to attend a pre-arranged event. A nice walk to the park or the shops is fine.

- If your child is active in the morning, it will be much easier to get him to take a long nap, preferably in his cot, in the afternoon.

Many children under 12 months will also need a short nap incorporated in to the mid-morning period and/or a longer one in the early afternoon. If you are out and about, try not to let him fall asleep in your arms during a feed, but lay him sleepily down awake in his pram.

Complete your routine planner in the workbook to include your chosen activities. You can download additional copies from the Baby Sleep Answers website if you need a separate routine for each day because the activity times are different, or you work on some days and not others.

3.5   The All Important Bedtime Routine

This is the most important part of your day. Get this bit right and you will be well on your way to a guaranteed full night's sleep. The Bedtime Routine must include a range of "sleep cues" that your baby or child will learn to recognise in a short period of time. Sleep cues are the things that you will do every night, to show your child that it is time for bed and sleep.

Here is a list of "sleep cues" that you can use. It is not exhaustive and you may develop some extra ones of your own:

- Bath

- Massage

- Dress in pyjamas

- Read a book or play a quiet game together

- Turn off main light and put on night light

- Activate musical mobile

- Same use of phrase such as "night, night sleep tight"

The routine should start at around 5:45pm but no later than 6:30pm. Run a nice warm bath and add a baby sleep time product. Make the bath fun. Dry the baby in his or her bedroom, massage him if you wish and put on a fresh nappy and a comfortable sleep suit. Give him a final milk feed and wind if necessary. It is important that all babies experience a gap, no matter how short, between the feed and going to bed. Read baby a story or play a lullaby. Turn the lights off and activate a musical mobile. Leave the room (this might not be possible immediately, see chapter 7 for more details). This routine should be the same every single night and last no longer than 45 minutes. The key point is that she goes down in her cot tired, but awake.

You should now have the details of your routine written in your workbook. Have a look at the *example* routines in the next chapter. Each part of the routine has specific advice on how to ensure success. The advice varies depending on the age of the child.

4 The Baby Sleep System: Example Routines

This section outlines some example routines that should be used for guidance only. By now you should have started to design your own routine in the Routine Planner section of the workbook. Study the example routine in this section that is suitable for a baby the same age as yours and check that you have met the basic principles.

4.1 New Babies Aged 0 – 6 weeks

No new baby can sleep through the night for the first few weeks after it is born. The size of the stomach is insufficient to hold enough milk to meet their needs for a 7 - 9 hour stretch. However, the key to getting your child to sleep through the night as early as possible is to introduce good sleep habits from day one. Even at this very early stage you can begin to teach your baby to settle himself without the need for contact with a parent, rocking or food.

Establishing a Daytime Routine

EXAMPLE of a daytime routine for a breast-fed baby aged 0 – 6 weeks

7:00am   Wake the baby if still sleeping
          Bottle or breastfeed
          Wind
          Change nappy and dress

9:00am	Feed and wind.
	Put the baby down awake in his crib while he is full and drowsy for a nap
11:00am	Feed
	Get out of the house. This could be a walk, a trip to a post natal group, the shops etc.
1:00pm	Feed
	Wind and change
	Put the baby down awake in his crib while he is full and drowsy for a nap
3:00pm	Feed
	Wind and change
	Put the baby down awake in his crib while he is full and drowsy for a nap
5:00pm	Feed
	Wind and change
5:45pm	Start Bedtime Routine:
	- Bath
	- Pyjamas
	- Move to bedroom
	- Dim the light
6:30pm -7:00pm	Tank Feed
	Play some soothing music or read a book
	Put the baby in the cot awake, but drowsy
	Activate musical mobile and leave

The routine outlined above is an example. Bottle fed babies may be able to go longer between feeds than breast fed babies for example. The aim of your routine should be to establish specific times for feeds and naps and to get your baby used to going down in his cot awake without the need for food, rocking or any other 'prop'.

Encouraging a Six Hour Sleep Window

For a new baby aged 0 – 6 weeks

10:30pm -11:00pm If you have not already done so, this is a good time to introduce the "tank up and dream feed" approach advocated by The Baby Whisperer Tracy Hogg (see Further Reading). Full details can be found in section 6.1 of the Night Feeds chapter.

A child of this age would be described as "sleeping through" from midnight until 6:00am. Some children do this at around 6 to 12 weeks old, but a crucial factor is birth weight. If a baby has a birth weight of 8 pounds or more at birth and continues to gain weight steadily, then they will have a greater capacity to fill themselves up and so sleep longer than a dainty 6 pounder. By sticking to the above principles your baby will sleep through when he is biologically ready to do so.

4.2   Babies Aged 6 weeks - 16 weeks

The routine set out below is an example and should be used for guidance only. If for instance you have other children in nursery and school, the timings will need to be "tweaked" to accommodate pick-ups, drop-offs etc. Try to keep the gaps between the feeds and naps consistent.

Establishing a Daytime Routine

EXAMPLE of a daytime routine for a baby aged 6 - 16 weeks

7:00am   Wake the baby if still sleeping
Bottle or breastfeed
Wind
Change nappy and dress

10:00am   Feed and wind.
Get out of the house. This could be a walk, a trip to a post natal group, the shops etc. If you follow this part of the routine every day your baby will nap in the pram.

1:00am   Feed followed by a short play
Put the baby down awake in his crib when he is tired for a nap

4:00pm   Feed
Wind, change and play
Put the baby down awake in his crib when he shows signs of tiredness

6:15pm   Start Bedtime Routine:
- Bath
- Pyjamas
- Move to bedroom
- Dim the light

7:00pm   Feed
Play some soothing music or read a book
Put the baby in the cot awake, but drowsy
Activate musical mobile and leave

Encouraging a Six Hour Sleep Window

For a baby aged 6 - 16 weeks

10:30pm If you have not already done so, and your baby is still
-11:00pm waking for a night feed, this is a good time to introduce the
"dream feed" advocated by *The Baby Whisperer* Tracy Hogg
(see Further Reading). Full details can be found in section
6.1 of the Night Feeds chapter.

4.3   Babies Aged 4 - 6 months

The example routine that follows is designed for babies aged between
4 - 6 months who have not yet been introduced to solid food.

Establishing a Daytime Routine

EXAMPLE of a daytime routine for a baby aged 4 - 6 months

7:00am   Wake up time
Bottle or breastfeed
Change nappy and dress

9:00am   Get out of the house. This could be a walk, a trip to a post
natal group, the shops etc.

9:30am   Nap (can be in the pushchair or car if out)

11:00am Feed

12:30pm Nap for 1½ - 2 hours

3:00pm	Feed
4:00pm	Catnap if needed (up to 1 hour)
6:45pm	Start Bedtime Routine:
	- Bath
	- Pyjamas
	- Move to bedroom
	- Dim the light
7:00pm	Feed
7:30pm	Put the baby in the cot awake
	Activate musical mobile and leave

Through the Night

For a baby aged 4 - 6 months

A baby of this age who is not weaned, may still need to feed during the night. However, he should not need milk more frequently than the time intervals established during the day.

Stick with or introduce a dream feed at 10:30-11:00. If your baby is in an established 4 hourly routine through the day, the next feed will then not be due until 2:30am-3:00am. The morning feed can be given between 6:30 and 7:00am. If need be, this morning feed can be given from 6:00am as this is in the normal waking range for a young baby.

If your baby wakes in between the times stated, offer cool boiled water and revert to one of the behaviour management techniques outlined in chapter 7.

If you are convinced that your baby really is very hungry during the night, consider offering him some solid food before the new 6 month recommended weaning age. This new advice has been issued by the World Health Organisation and needs to be put in context. The main aim is to reduce the risk of children developing food allergies which can be more likely if children are exposed to certain foods before the age of 6 months (and in certain instances 12 months). Furthermore, the recommendation is aimed at all babies throughout the world, including poor countries where food is often scarce and unsafe. The advice also takes no account of birth weight and growth which obviously has an impact on how many calories a baby needs to take, in order to feel full and grow. A baby on the 90th percentile is clearly going to need solid food before a child on the 9th and he may need it before 6 months!

Use your initiative and common sense. If your baby is bigger than average, appears hungry very soon after a big milk feed (through the day and at night), has started waking at night when he used to sleep, then consider introducing some solid meals from 16 weeks onwards. Stick to baby rice mixed with formula or breast milk and mashed up fruit and vegetables until he is 6 months old. By taking this simple step, the risk of allergy is completely minimised.

4.4   Babies Aged 6 - 9 months

As for all routines in this chapter, what follows is an example only and the timings should be used as a rough guide. By this stage all healthy babies should be eating a varied, solid diet in addition to their milk.

Establishing a Daytime Routine

EXAMPLE of a daytime routine for a baby aged 6 - 9 months

7:00am   Wake the baby if still sleeping
Bottle or breastfeed
Bowl of solid breakfast
Change nappy and dress

9:00am   Get out of the house. This could be a walk, a trip to a post natal group, the shops etc.

9:45am   Drink of milk/snack and change. Put down for a nap. If you are still out on your 'trip' put the baby down for sleep in his pram for no longer than 30 minutes - 1 hour.

12:00pm Solid lunch and change
-1:00pm   Put him down for a nap. Wake him up after 1½ - 2 hours

3:00pm   Drink of milk

4:15pm   If he is really tired, put him down for a nap, 30 - 45 minutes

5:30pm   Solid dinner and water or juice

babysleepanswers.co.uk

6:15pm	Start Bedtime Routine:
	- Bath
	- Pyjamas
	- Move to bedroom
	- Dim the light
7:00pm	Large bottle of milk (aim for 7ozs) or long breast feed from both sides
	Play some soothing music or read a book
7:30pm	Put the baby in the cot awake
	Activate musical mobile and leave

Through the Night

For a baby aged 6 - 9 months

A baby of this age does not need a milk feed through the night in order to grow and develop. Try ignoring him for a little while and see if he goes back to sleep on his own. Offer him boiled water as an alternative to milk. Have another look at what he is eating and drinking during the day and increase this if necessary (adding another course to main meals is often an easy way of doing this e.g. cheese and crackers, a banana). If you are really unsure about whether he is hungry, introduce a dream feed at 10:30 – 11:00.

If he continues to wake you will need to adopt one of the behaviour management techniques outlined in chapter 7.

4.5   Babies Aged 9 - 12 months

At this age many babies start to drop their morning nap. If he begins to fight the nap after lunch, then start to reduce the morning nap by 5 - 10 minutes a day. A catnap in the late afternoon should also no longer be necessary. Again as for all routines in this chapter, what follows is an example only and the timings should be used as a rough guide.

Establishing a Daytime Routine

EXAMPLE of a daytime routine for a baby aged 9 - 12 months

7:00am   Wake the baby if still sleeping
Bottle or breastfeed
Bowl of solid breakfast
Change nappy and dress

9:00am   Get out of the house. This could be a walk, a trip to a post natal group, the shops etc.

9:45am   Drink of milk/snack and change. Put down for a nap awake, but drowsy. If you are still out on your 'trip' put the baby down for a sleep in his pram for no longer than 30 minutes.

12:00pm Solid lunch and change

12:30pm Put him down for a nap, awake but drowsy. Wake him up after two and a half hours if necessary

3:00pm   Drink of milk

5:30pm   Solid Tea and water or juice

6:15pm   Start Bedtime Routine:
          - Bath
          - Pyjamas
          - Move to bedroom
          - Dim the light

7:00pm   Large bottle of milk (aim for 7ozs) or long breast feed from both sides
          Play some soothing music or read a book

7:30pm   Put the baby in the cot awake, but drowsy
          Activate musical mobile and leave

Through the Night

For a baby aged 9 - 12 months

A baby of this age does not need a milk feed through the night in order to grow and develop. Try ignoring him for a little while and see if he goes back to sleep on his own. Offer him boiled water as an alternative to milk. Have another look at what he is eating and drinking during the day and increase this if necessary (adding another course to main meals is often an easy way of doing this e.g. cheese and crackers, a banana).

If he continues to wake you will need to adopt one of the behaviour management techniques outlined in chapter 7.

4.6 Babies and Children Aged 12 Months And Over

This routine is suitable for all children over 12 months old. By 2 years, some children no longer need an afternoon nap that lasts for 2 hours and by 3 years of age most will have dropped this sleep altogether. If your child is over 2 and is still not sleeping through the night, an integral part of your strategy should be to stop the afternoon nap. In any event do not let your child take a nap after 4:00pm as this will impact on the night-time sleep.

Establishing a Daytime Routine

EXAMPLE of a daytime routine for a child aged 12 months +

7:00am   Wake the baby if he is still sleeping. Bottle or breastfeed him and serve some breakfast e.g. cereal or toast. Change his nappy and dress.

9:00am   Get out of the house. This could be a walk, a trip to a friend, the shops, a mother and baby group etc.

10:00am Give the baby a drink and a snack and change if necessary. Play time.

12:30pm Serve lunch, change if required
Bring this lunchtime forward if he is struggling to stay awake

1:00pm   Put him down for a nap, awake but drowsy. Wake him after two and a half hours if necessary.

3.00pm   Drink of milk

5:30pm   Solid Tea and water or juice

6:15pm   Start Bedtime Routine:
- Bath
- Pyjamas
- Move to bedroom
- Dim the light

7:00pm   Large bottle of milk (aim for 7ozs) or long breast feed from both sides
Play some soothing music or read a book

7:30pm   Put the baby in the cot awake, but drowsy
Activate musical mobile and leave

Through the Night

For a child aged 12 months +

A child of this age does not need a milk feed through the night in order to grow and develop. Try ignoring him for a little while and see if he goes back to sleep on his own. Offer him boiled water as an alternative to milk. Have another look at what he is eating and drinking during the day and increase this if necessary (adding another course to main meals is often an easy way of doing this e.g. cheese and crackers, a banana).

If he continues to wake you will need to adopt one of the behaviour management techniques outlined in chapter 7.

4.7　Now it's Your Turn!

Now that you have devised your routine, you can begin to implement it during the day. The next section will help you to settle your baby into the naps that are a vital part of your new plan.

5   Naps

Why are naps so important? As ridiculous as it sounds more sleep in the day equals more sleep at night. Therefore before moving on to sorting out poor bedtime behaviour and night waking, we must first address poor napping during the day. The table in section 2.3 gives details of the number of naps that are appropriate for different aged children. Section 3.3 provides information about the timing of these.

5.1   Causes of a Poor Nap Routine

Short naps or no napping during the day often happens for the following reasons:

1. Poor Routine
Babies who have never had a set routine imposed by their parents, are not able to settle into the pattern which nature intended. They therefore have to re-learn the skills that they did not develop.

2. Sleep Cycle Interruption
Sometimes in the effort to be a nurturing parent, mum or dad has dashed in at the first sign of waking. The baby has therefore got used to having a short nap. A slight delay would have allowed him to go back off to sleep for the appropriate length of time.

3. Overtired

Once a baby starts to display signs of being tired, the nap window has opened. At the first indication of nap readiness e.g. eye rubbing, ear pulling or face scratching your baby needs to be put in his bed.

4. Over Stimulation

Just like at night, a wind down period is necessary before she is put in her cot. It does not need to be a long and drawn out ritual; quiet play, a drink and snuggle, a musical mobile or a quick book can really help to set the scene.

If problem napping is deeply rooted in your baby, you may need to follow the above and adopt a more proactive approach. The next section explains how to help your baby to nap.

5.2 Building Naps into the Routine

5.2.1 Settling For a Nap

It can be difficult to get your baby to nap, especially in the early days of a new routine. Initially it is better to concentrate on the main nap of the day, which is usually taken just after lunch. Set your "sleep window", initially this should be an hour. Use pick up/put down (PUPD) or pick up/put down/cry down (PUPDCD) for the entire window (see section 7) or until your baby falls asleep. If she falls asleep, great, do not worry too much about the length of the nap. At this stage it is more important that she has fallen asleep on her own in the cot.

If she does not fall asleep, wait for a time until she looks like she is going to nod off and try again. If she waits for the next feed to fall asleep, rouse her before putting her down in the cot. She does not have to be wide awake, but drowsy.

After a few days, the process will get easier and she will start to settle better in her cot and fall asleep on her own.

Try to avoid letting a baby over six months old fall asleep after 4:30 in the afternoon as it will impact on her night's sleep. However, you can put her to bed from 6:15pm. She may well wake earlier, but this can be dealt with later.

5.2.2   Extending Naps

If she wakes too early from the nap (less than half an hour for morning naps, and less than one and a half hours in the afternoon) then you can use pick up/put down to get her back to sleep. However, do not dash in to pick her up too soon, leave her for 10 minutes, you may find that she settles herself back off to sleep on her own. As a general rule of thumb, if she wakes early and is crying, she is still tired and needs to get back to sleep.

The next section will look at the issue of feeding. Again it is important that this is sorted out, as it is essential to dealing successfully with the night time problems.

Case Study: Claire and William

Claire and her 10 month old son William live in Harrogate, North Yorkshire. William had not been a good sleeper and his parents had never had a full night's sleep since the day he was born. By the time Claire purchased The Baby Sleep System he was getting gradually worse. William was sleeping in his parents' bed for most of the time especially after 10:00pm and waking every hour. Claire was determined to break the cycle and was keen to get started with the programme.

The Strategy

I helped Claire to devise a routine that incorporated the right number of naps in the correct places. We all agreed that William must be banished from his parents' bed. Once these rules had been established we worked on a strategy to deal with the night time waking. Claire was advised to post on the Baby Sleep Answers forum everyday to get up to date advice and much needed support.

The Result

There were a few blips along the way, but within two weeks William was sleeping in his own bed for the whole night.

As Claire put it in her most recent post on the forum:

"Hi again Wendy, well you were right by Friday night he was sleeping straight through without even waking once so this is brilliant and he has kept it up so far, he even goes to sleep now without any crying and is usually asleep within 5 minutes so that is great … Plus we finally have a bed to ourselves and most importantly get a full night's sleep. I know there will probably be some hiccups along the way but it is looking really good."

6   Night Feeds

Most babies are capable of sleeping for a six hour stretch from around six weeks old. This is described by many parents as "sleeping through" if they do not have to get up between midnight and 6:00am.

6.1   Encouraging a Six Hour Sleep Window

To maximise your chances of achieving the window, try the "tanking approach" recommended by Tracy Hogg, the Baby Whisperer. Babies between 0 and 6 weeks should be fed at two hour intervals in the early evening at 5.00pm and 7.00pm or 6.00pm and 8.00pm. Baby should then be put in her cot awake. Between 10.00pm and 11.00pm the baby can then be lifted from her cot and given a dream feed. This feed can sometimes be given while the baby is still asleep. If not, gently wake her. You should keep the bedroom light off, wiggle the teat of the bottle into her mouth if bottle feeding or stroke the bottom lip with your little finger if breast feeding to start the sucking reflex.

Some babies are harder to tank up than others. If you cannot get your baby to tank up and dream feed, just opt for the dream feed (which can be continued until 7 or 8 months old). Once your child is consistently sleeping until 6.00am, drop the tanking and gradually bring the dream feed back by 15 minutes until you reach 9:00pm. It can then be omitted altogether.

Make sure you record on your Routine Planner, the time where you will tank and dream feed.

6.2   When to Stop Night Time Feeding

This is a question that is asked very frequently. As a general rule of thumb, you can stop feeding your baby between midnight and 6.00am when one of the following happens:

1. Your baby reaches the age of 6-7 months and is eating solid food over three meals a day.

2. During the night feeds she drinks less than 3oz of formula or nurses for less than 5 minutes.

3. You are feeding her every four hours during the day, are tanking and/or dream feeding, she is over 4 months old and wakes at exactly the same time every night.

If you are considering stopping night feeds and your baby is under 6 months old, consult with your Health Visitor or post on the Baby Sleep Answers forum. There may be other things that you can try before having to resort to a behaviour management strategy.

6.3   How to Stop Night Time Feeds?

Once you have established that your baby no longer needs a feed during the night, you can choose whether to stop feeding him completely and go straight to using a behaviour management technique or you can wean your child off the milk gradually.

6.3.1 The Milk Reduction Approach

Dr. Richard Ferber, the author of *Solve Your Child's Sleep Problems: A Practical and Comprehensive Guide for Parents*, suggests a tried and tested method for weaning baby off the breast or the bottle in the middle of the night.

Breast feeding mothers should start by reducing the length of the feed by one minute. Over a few days reduce the time of the feeds until they are only a minute in duration. At this point the baby is ready to begin one of the behaviour management sleep training techniques set out below. If possible somebody other than the mother should do the checking or support the baby for the first five nights whilst sleep training.

Bottle feeding parents can start by reducing the amount of milk by one fluid ounce a night. When the feeds are down to four fluid ounces, parents can choose to continue to reduce the amount over a further three nights or start to dilute the milk by adding less powder (this should only be done as part of this night time strategy for a short period). Once down to one fluid ounce or extremely dilute milk, then one of the behaviour management strategies set out below can be invoked.

6.3.2 The Calorie Maximisation Approach

This method can be used for babies over 4 months old who are on the 25th or above percentile for their age and weight.

The dream feed can be left as it is to start with. No feeds should be given within four 4 hours following the dream feed e.g. if the dream feed was given at 11:00pm, the baby will not need another feed until 3:00am. The next feed will then be 7:00am. You may need to use one of the behaviour management strategies outlined in section 7 in order to achieve this.

Once the baby has maintained the 3:00am only feed for one week, this can then be diluted down or stopped and the next feed can be given at 6:00am. At this stage, it is not advisable to feed baby before 6:00am as this will encourage early waking (see section 8.2 for more information).

Make sure you record your night feed times on your Routine Planner in the workbook.

6.3.3 Dropping the Dream Feed

Once your baby has slept through the night solidly for six full weeks, you may want to consider dropping the dream feed in order to achieve a 12 hour stretch of solid sleep. You can opt for one of two choices:

1. Take a chance and stop offering him the milk. With luck, he may not wake and will sleep through to the morning. If this does not happen, you can always re-introduce the dream feed.

2. Move the feed by 15 minutes each night over a few nights until you reach 9:00pm. If your baby has continued to not wake, then drop the feed completely.

The Baby Sleep System

If you opt for this approach you can use the Routine Planner to record your times over the next few days.

6.4   Additional Feeding Tips

It may still be possible to avoid a full scale sleep training plan. Have a quick recap of the following checklist, to make sure that you have not missed a simple solution:

1. Is he taking enough food at each sitting? By 4 months an average baby should be taking a minimum of a 5 ounce bottle in one feed. If your baby's weight is above average then consider giving him a bit more.

2. Breast fed babies sometimes do not get enough milk at the last feed, especially if their mother is exhausted. Consider topping him up with a few ounces of formula or express more milk off in the morning to give him via a bottle in the evening.

3. Although the latest advice is to not wean (introduce solid food) a baby until he is six months old, use your own judgement. If your baby is above average weight then he may be ready at four months old (see section 3.2 for more information). Remember, it is your baby and you know him best.

If you are confident that you have now tried everything in this section and your baby is still not sleeping through the night, it is time to progress to a sleep training programme. The next section will take you through a number of options and you can choose which one you would like to adopt.

babysleepanswers.co.uk

45

Case Study: Ann and Alexander

Ann and her son Alexander (16 weeks old) live in Oslo, Norway. Ann heard about Baby Sleep Answers through an article featuring the site in Practical Parenting Magazine. Ann was breastfeeding Alexander every three hours during the day and on demand at night and had just introduced him to solids for one meal a day.

Alexander slept erratically during the day and as a result his daytime routine was unpredictable. His bedtime routine was excellent and he fell asleep at night with no problems. However, he woke anytime between 11:00pm and 2:00am for a feed and then every two to three hours after that.

By the time Ann made her first post on the Baby Sleep Answers forum she was totally exhausted and had developed Post Natal Depression. She had tried other books claiming to help babies sleep better, but they had not worked for Alexander.

The Strategy

I explained to Ann that a four month old baby can do a longer stretch of sleep through the night than her little man was currently doing.

The first course of action that Ann and I decided to embark on was to get Alexander into a solid daytime routine. Feeds and naps would be taken at the right time and be for an appropriate length. I explained that as Alexander was now four months old he needed to be on a four rather than a three hour feeding routine. A four month old baby who is on a three hourly routine often has irregular naps and wakes in the night. At this point the routine needed to incorporate two good naps (two hours each) and a cat nap.

Once we had designed a suitable programme, Ann elected to use controlled crying and pick up/put down to settle Alexander into it. I also recommended getting rid of Alexander's dummy right at the start of the process.

At first, getting Alexander into the new routine was very difficult. He was waking too early from his naps and because he was still tired and unhappy about his new routine, he cried a lot.

Ann used the forum to get additional advice and extra support on a daily basis. Other users of the System offered her encouragement as well as me. Gradually over a couple of weeks Alexander's day time sleep patterns began to improve.

The next stage was to address the night time waking. We had another look at his routine during the night and took action including increasing his calories during the day to extend his sleep window.

The Result

A few weeks later Ann reported the following:

"Alexander turned 20 weeks old on Tuesday and I can honestly say, hand on heart, that this week has been a joy and for the first time I've really enjoyed being his mum. He naps like a dream during the day, either in his cot or in his pram (I make sure that one of the naps is at home), he is a much more contented baby and I'm a much more contented mum. I don't feel so overwhelmed by the PND anymore and now have the energy to deal with it.

My husband and I are also rediscovering one another again and spending quality time together. I'm under no illusions that there won't be blips along the way and that I'll come back for more advice but in the meantime, thank you from the bottom of heart. You have no idea what your advice and support has meant to our family. You are one of a kind, Wendy Dean. A big hug from me."

7 Managing Bedtimes and Night-time Waking

There are a range of techniques that can be employed to get your child to sleep through the night. Those described in the Baby Sleep System all fall under the general heading of behaviour management approaches. Some of the methods do entail leaving your child to cry for short periods. Others are "no cry".

The method you choose is really down to your parenting style and personal preferences. See if you can identify what sort of parent you are from the following descriptions. For each type, there is a suggested technique which you might find suits you the best.

1. The Emotional Parent
   You really cannot face leaving your child to cry for any length of time and are prepared to put a massive amount of time and effort into ensuring that this does not happen. You are not in a great hurry to have a full night's sleep and are prepared to make sacrifices such as implementing the method without a partners support and move out of your own bedroom.

   Suggested method: Continuous Pick Up/Put Down (PUPD) or Gradual Withdrawal

2. The Pragmatic Parent
   You do not want to leave your child for an extended period to cry, but would consider short breaks. You want to follow a loose

structure which includes a variety of different methods to comfort your child.

Suggested method: Pick Up/Put Down/Cry Down (PUPDCD)

3. The End of the Line Parent
    You are happy to work to a pre-designed plan and stick to it. You would rather opt for an effective strategy that will work as quickly as possible. You are prepared to put up with a lot of tears as long as you know you will see an improvement within a week.

    Suggested method: Controlled Crying (CC)

4. The Fun Parent
    You are the parent of an older child (over 18 months) who cannot leave him/her to cry for any period of time. You are happy to devote a lot of time in the evening and through the night to help your child settle and have an infinite amount of patience.

    Suggested method: The Kissing Game

5. The Negotiating Parent
    You are the parent of a child over two and a half. She understands the concepts of rewards and sanctions. You are happy to establish a chart and a series of treats and penalties. You do not want to use any method which involves physically moving your child or that will result in more than 10 minutes of crying.

    Suggested method: The Carrot and Stick Approach

6. The Authority Parent

You have an older child who is sleeping in a bed and is mobile. You have come to the end of your tether and feel that it is time to set some bed and night-time boundaries. You are prepared to be absolutely consistent for two weeks.

Suggested method: Back to Bed, Closed Door Technique, Barrier Method

7.1   Safety First

It is absolutely imperative before starting any sleep training method, that you follow the guidelines below:

- Fully satisfy yourself that your baby is not ill. Check for rashes and take a temperature reading
- Check the cot for unsafe items such as sharp puzzles, toys with string or cord attached etc.
- Make sure that there are locks on older children's windows (hide the keys in a safe place in the room in case there is a fire)
- Use a baby monitor set at low volume

Feel confident that the cot and the room is a safe zone for your child.

7.1.1 Option 1 – Pick Up / Put Down (PUPD)

This no cry method was pioneered by Tracy Hogg, otherwise known as *The Baby Whisperer*. It can take quite a long time, but if you are committed it will work.

The method allows you to stay with your child, but she will still learn to go to sleep without having to rely on you. It is suitable for babies from birth to around seven months who have not learnt how to fall asleep on their own.

The method is hard work and is easier if two people take it in turns. Follow these steps and keep it up for as long as it takes:

1. When baby cries go into her room. First try to comfort her with words and gentle head stroking.

2. If she doesn't stop crying pick her up. Say "shush, shush" and gently pat her back.

3. As soon as she stops crying, put her down immediately.

4. You are not rocking her to sleep, you are aiming to get her to fall asleep in her cot.

5. If she is crying and arching her back in your arms, put her back down immediately. It can be very dangerous to get into a fight with a baby.

6. While she is in the cot, place one hand on the top of her head and the other on her chest. Speak to her as well e.g. "go to sleep mummy is here".

7. Even if she cries the minute that she starts to descend into her cot, put her all the way to the mattress before you pick her up again.

8. Remember if she is arching her back, put her back in. This is actually her way of starting to go to sleep.

9. If you do pick up/put down correctly i.e. pick her up when she cries and put her down the minute she stops, she will eventually run out of steam and cry less.

10. Once she is lying in the cot and is quiet she will be about to go to sleep. Stay with her with your hand firmly placed on her body, the pressure and reassuring words will let her know that you are still there. Do not leave the room until you are certain that she is in deep sleep.

11. Later on she will go straight down into her cot and will be reassured by your voice alone.

Tracy Hogg maintained in her book, *The Baby Whisperer Solves all Your Problems*, that this method takes on average 20 minutes. In my experience it is not usually as quick as this and with a feistier baby can take up to two hours. Be prepared to pick your baby up between 50 and 250 times.

As mentioned earlier, this method has been marketed as a no cry solution. This is not entirely accurate, because as you can see some crying is involved. However, you are able to stay in the room and support your baby which some parents find comforting. Dealing with a crying baby is very difficult and you should not feel guilty. You are not hurting her, you are helping her. She is crying because she is frustrated and doesn't know how to fall asleep.

7.1.2 Option 2 – Pick Up/Put Down/Cry Down (PUPDCD)

This method is suitable for babies from six weeks old to around nine months. You help and support your baby to learn how to fall asleep, but breaks are built in to allow your child to "cry down" and to help you cope. It is based on a three phase approach.

Phase 1

PUPD for 20 minutes. If he does not cry (unlikely to begin with) then leave him in the cot and busy yourself around the room. If he cries pick him up, say, "shush, shush" and pat his back. When he stops crying put him down. If he starts crying on the down, lower him to the mattress before you pick him up. After 20 minutes, put him in the cot and leave him for 10 minutes. Repeat for a further 20 minutes and then put him in the cot for 10 minutes. You can stay with him for the breaks, but this approach generally works better if you leave the room. If he is still crying, repeat phase 1 a second time.

Phase 2

If he has "cried down" – he may still be crying a bit, but not with the same intensity - stroke his head gently for 15 minutes, leave the room for 10 minutes and then repeat for a further five minutes or until he falls asleep (whichever is the sooner). If he is still awake after the 2nd hair stroking, move to phase 3.

Phase 3

If he is still not asleep after phase 2, leave the room for five minutes. Go back in and stroke his hair, say "night, night" and leave for a further five minutes and so on until he falls asleep.

You need to do this for three nights. After this you should begin to see a real improvement.

7.1.3 Option 3 – Controlled Crying

This approach has received a lot of bad press over the last few years. This has mainly come from sections of the parenting press who advocate that babies should never have a reason to cry. If they are left to do so it is psychologically damaging. There is absolutely no scientific evidence to support this. As long as your baby is loved and well cared for, sleep training using the controlled crying method will help him to be a healthier and happier child.

Certainly my own experience has shown that often, by the time parents seek help for their disturbed sleep, they are at the end of their tether. Many mothers have developed post-natal depression and the problem has serious implications for the family as a unit and the adult relationship. What parents want and need is a quick solution. My experience of working with thousands of families generally indicates that the controlled crying approach will give you the quickest results, but may involve quite a lot of tears. It is not suitable for babies under the age of four months.

If you do decide to go down this route a report in the **British Medical Journal** found that teaching mothers controlled crying techniques significantly reduced sleep problems. Mothers who learn to let their babies cry themselves to sleep have better nights and suffer less postnatal depression.

Randomised controlled trial of behavioural infant sleep intervention to improve infant sleep and maternal mood. H Hiscock & M Wake BMJJournals.com *BMJ* 2002;**324**;1062.doi:10.1136/bmj.324.7345.1062

The controlled crying technique is very effective and you should see a dramatic improvement within 3 - 10 days. However, it must be implemented correctly and consistently. The following sections list the key things to do and remember.

Putting Your Child to Bed
Put your baby in his cot fully awake, say a key phrase e.g. "night night", activate the musical mobile and leave the room. It does not matter if he stands up in his cot. The whole point is that you are teaching him to get himself off to sleep.

Controlling the Crying
The "controlled" bit of controlled crying is the subsequent checking. In order to help you be successful, follow the tips below:

Be Prepared: Agree with your partner that you are *both* going to stick to the controlled crying regime for one week. Each must help the other not to cave in.

Use a baby monitor: This way you can distance yourself from the crying, but have the volume turned just high enough so that you can check your child is safe.

Planning the checking: will help you to carry it through. Write down the time when you will be starting, e.g. 7:00pm, and the times that you intend to check back. You should start by checking every five minutes for the first 15 minutes. For the next 30 minutes, you check on him every 10 minutes. For the next half an hour, every 15 minutes and so on until he has gone to sleep. Writing it down and ticking each check off will really help you to cope.

During the checking: When you do the checking, try not to give him too much attention. Use one or two sleep cues, e.g. reset the mobile, or quietly say the key phrase and then walk out of the room. Leave the light off. Some children become more wound up by the sight of their parent. In these circumstances, peek around the door so that he cannot see you.

You Are Doing The Right Thing!

Your baby will cry, perhaps hysterically, the first few times that you do this and may stand up. Do not give up. You will not be risking any kind of attachment problems (see 2.4.3) provided that you are consistent in the way that you respond. Remember that parents have to help their baby to learn how to regulate stressful situations and cope with changes. Controlled crying, when carried out correctly, does help to do this. You are not psychologically damaging him. This technique has been used for many, many years and you are not the first to be going through the heartbreak. The long term benefits of establishing a proper sleep pattern far outweigh the short term angst. Understand why he is crying; he liked the old way of falling asleep. In the morning you will be greeted by a happy, smiling baby who still loves you.

7.1.4 Option 4 – The Kissing Game

This approach is suggested by Penny Hames in her book, Help Your Baby to Sleep (see Further Reading) and is particularly good for children aged between 18 months and two years and pre-schoolers that refuse to sleep. It also gives parents who cannot let their children "cry it out" another option. Again it is vitally important to have a good routine during the day (including naps for younger children) and a very consistent bedtime routine.

Putting Your Child to Bed

Kiss your child goodnight and promise to return in 1 minute to give him another kiss. Return almost immediately and kiss him again. Move a few steps away and then go back and kiss him. Put some washing or toys away and kiss him again. Step outside for a few seconds and dash back in to kiss him again. Go downstairs and come back up to plant another kiss.

The aim is to leave slightly longer gaps between the kisses. Do not chat, provide drinks or do anything else except kiss him. The only rule is that the child must stay in his bed with his head on the pillow. Don't shout if he gets out of bed, just reinforce the rule "bed = kisses". You might have to give up to 500 kisses on the first few nights. If you find this amount of kissing a bit difficult, substitute the kiss for a pat.

7.1.5 Option 5 – Gradual Withdrawal

This is the option for parents who do not want their children to cry at all and again is featured in Help Your Baby to Sleep. It works on the principle that you can gradually distance yourself from your child and still let them learn to fall asleep on their own. Again I would suggest that this strategy needs to be combined with a good solid bedtime routine.

Putting Your Child to Bed

Start by lying down with the baby until he goes to sleep. After a couple of nights or however long it takes for your child to feel comfortable with it, move to the edge of the bed. After another appropriate period, move to a chair by the side of the bed. Then move the chair little by little across the room taking as long as your child needs. Sit outside the door for a few evenings so you can respond if he calls to you. Each position could take two or three nights – do not rush it.

If your child cries in the night you must repeat the process from the position that your child is comfortable with; i.e. you may have to lie with him or he might be comfortable with you sitting by the door.

7.2　Additional Advice for Parents of Older Children

The principles that have been set out in the earlier sections of this chapter remain the same for older children as they do for babies.

Daytime Routines

Daytime routines need to be consistent, but there is more of a need to build in opportunities for physical exercise, e.g. a walk to the park or a session in an indoor play area.

Bedtime Routines

Television should not be allowed after 7:00pm and it is not advisable to have a TV, computer or any electronic games in the bedroom. Do not be sidetracked and do not give in to demands to stay up later, watch TV, avoid the bath or the story etc. Give your child cues that bedtime is approaching so that it does not come as a surprise e.g. after we have read this story, you are going to get in bed and go to sleep. At the appropriate hour make it absolutely clear that it is bedtime and that the child is going to bed. Make sure that the bedtime routine is fun. Overlook minor misdemeanours at the bath and story stage.

7.3　Keeping Your Child in Bed

In many respects it is harder to get an older child to go to sleep and then remain that way for the whole night. Babies, for example, are already confined by a cot. Parents with older children in a bed will inevitably find that their child keeps getting out. Consider doing the following:

7.3.1　Option 1 – Carrot And Stick Approach

Older children often respond well to a wide variety of incentive schemes and this type of approach should be tried first. Here are a few suggestions:

Sticker or Star Chart

This can work particularly well if you are trying to sleep train more than one child. Competing with a sibling can be a very powerful tool. Be absolutely clear about what the children have to do to receive a star e.g. remaining in bed. Set out at the beginning what the reward will be if they get say 3 stars. If either child does not stay in bed then they must not get their star. Be absolutely consistent; do not change the goal posts.

Rewards and Two Jars

This is a very good time limited incentive scheme. Set a time period with your child (it could be a week, 3 days or 1 night). Half fill two jars with exactly the same number of sweets or small toys. Label one jar with 'good' and the other 'naughty'. If the child behaves at bath time take one sweet from the naughty jar and put it in the 'good' jar or vice versa. Repeat the exercise for each part of the bedtime routine. At the end of your set time period, the child gets all of the contents of the 'good' jar.

Using Toys

Have a good sort out of all your child's toys and reduce the number to around 10 particular favourites. Put the rest in a place where they cannot be accessed. Put the toys in a basket. If the child sticks to his bedtime routine, then he can play with all the toys. If he is badly behaved at any point in the routine then he loses a toy. The following night, if he behaves he gets that toy back etc. This strategy has knock-on benefits in that toys suddenly become cherished and played with, rather than the majority being unloved and ignored at the bottom of a toy box.

Time Rewards

Rewards do not necessarily have to be toys or sweets, treats involving your time can be more effective. Here are some examples:

- Playing with play dough
- Going for a picnic
- Reading a story with Mummy or Daddy
- Watching a video
- A trip to the playground
- A trip to the park

7.3.2 Option 2 – Back to Bed

If your child has not responded to the carrot and stick approach, you may wish to consider taking a firmer line. The back to bed approach involves the parent enforcing the instruction to "stay in bed" and is used in conjunction with one of the behaviour management strategies set out above.

Make sure that your child is quite clear about what it is you want him to do. If he gets out lead him back without comment. If you are following the gradual withdrawal or kissing game strategies carry on as if nothing has happened. If you are following controlled crying wait outside the bedroom door as you will need to respond quickly to the next attempt to get out of bed.

Be absolutely consistent, if he gets out of bed, put him back in. Try not to shout and use the minimum amount of strength necessary to get him back into bed. Do not get into a physical "fight" with your child. If the situation is getting out of hand, adopt option 3 below.

7.3.3 Option 3 – Closed Door Technique

Put your child back to bed and say that you are going to close the door for 1 minute. If he is still in bed after this time, you will open it again.

Open the door and if he is still in bed leave it open. If he has got out re-issue the instruction, but say that this time you are going to close the door for 2 minutes. Continue until he remains in bed.

There is a possibility that you could end up fighting over the door with your toddler or pre-schooler. Remind yourself that you are the adult and therefore the one in control. This child needs his sleep and so as long as you know that your child is safe, use your strength to keep the door closed.

7.3.4 Option 4 – Barrier Method

Use a stair gate to ensure your child is confined to his bedroom and to make sure that he cannot embark on dangerous night time wanderings. It can also be used to enforce controlled crying. If your child falls asleep on the floor, it can be distressing, but at least he has learnt to fall asleep on his own!

You may start with controlled crying for the first 2 or 3 nights and then move on to carrot and stick later when you child has realised that you are serious about the new rule that he has to stay in his bed.

7.3.5 Six Point Plan to Success

In summary, although getting an older child to sleep through can be more challenging and take longer than for a baby, it is also possible to use your negotiation skills to better effect. At least you can explain to an older child what it is that you want and you can offer rewards. As a result you may experience less guilty feelings than those parents who are trying to 'teach' a small baby. To hammer the point home, make sure that you stick to the two key underlining principles:

Clear Rules and Boundaries

Be sure that your child fully understands what you want him to do. Make sure he fully understands what will happen if he does or does not do this. Follow through i.e. give the reward or give the sanction exactly as you had laid it out at the beginning.

Pleasant Bedroom

Do not use the bedroom or cot as a place of punishment. If during the day, your child is naughty, do not send him to his bedroom or put him in his cot. Use another room, a playpen or a naughty step. Make your child's bedroom an attractive place to be.

Hopefully you have now decided which of the techniques you want to start with. You may decide to switch to another approach one you get underway. For example, some parents find that pick up/put down (PUPD) is too stimulating for their child at 3:00am but works well for afternoon naps. Add your selection to your Routine Planner (see the example in the workbook). Remember you can always download extra workbook sheets if you adapt your plan from the website.

Read The Six Point Plan to Success and you are nearly ready to begin.

The Six Point Plan to Success
1 Keep a sleep diary the week before you begin so you can monitor your progress.
2 Pick a time to begin when it does not matter If you are more tired the next day e.g. start on a Friday night.
3 Agree your goal e.g. fall asleep on his own, stay in bed, sleep through without a feed etc.
4 Explain your goal and your approach to the child if he is old enough to understand.
5 Tell the neighbours what you are doing, particularly if you are anticipating a lot of tears.
6 Keep a record of progress in the workbook so that you can see even small improvements.

Case Study: Rachel and Bobbie

Rachel and her daughter Bobbie, live in Reading, Berkshire. At 24 weeks old Rachel started Bobbie on The Baby Sleep System. She was on three meals a day of fruit and vegetables and had a 5 ounce bottle at bedtime. The remainder of the daytime feeds and all of the night time feeds were taken from the breast. She was a healthy full term baby who was growing well.

Rachel was becoming exhausted. Bobbie was waking sometimes 15 to 20 times a night and four or five times a night between 1:00am and 6:30am.

"Sleep deprivation seems to make everything worse and makes you lose confidence in your ability to carry this sleep training out! I am sure I am not alone in this but it is hard not to think that at 3:00 in the morning!"

The Strategy

After working with Rachel through The Baby Sleep Answers forum over a couple of sessions, we established that the key problems with Bobby's sleep were:

1. She had a good sleep in the morning (about an hour) in the car or pushchair and was quite happy to do this without crying or need for the dummy. However, she would not sleep in her cot in the afternoon. The conclusion was that she had incorporated a rocking motion into her sleep strategy. This is probably part of the reason why she was not going down awake in her cot without a lot of protest.

2. She was using a dummy to get herself off to sleep at night - if it fell out she woke up.

Once the key problems had been identified then a strategy was drawn up:

1. It was decided that if at all possible Bobbie was to take an afternoon sleep. Contrary to common sense more sleep in the afternoon equals more sleep at night. We aimed for a sleep from 12:30 (straight after lunch) until around 2:30 as the ideal.

2. Rachel was directed to the Baby Sleep Answers website to download the article on ditching the dummy in 5 easy steps.

3. We then looked at which strategy Rachel was going to select from The Baby Sleep System to deal with the resistance that her baby put up every time she was put in her cot. Rachel was particularly concerned about leaving her baby to cry, as she put it:

"She hasn't really had anything to cry about for the first 6 months of her life and now all of a sudden I am inflicting it on her."

I reassured her that she needed to make sure that her baby wasn't crying for any other reason other than not wanting to go to sleep e.g. she was not hungry, too hot, too cold or ill. I then referred her to the medical papers at the news section of The Baby Sleep Answers website. This includes a number of articles that demonstrate that poor sleeping habits are a much greater risk to physical and psychological health than leaving a baby to cry for a short time.

As I explained, even the so called "no cry" strategies contained in The Baby Sleep System (and other baby sleep books on the market), usually result in a few tears. Her baby needed her support to learn to go to sleep but Rachel could not do this for her.

The Result

A few weeks later Rachel reported the following:

"I have been carrying out your sleep system for the last three weeks and have great results to report. My baby is now 28 weeks old, sleeping in her own room, without being swaddled and without the dummy. It took us a while but we have got there and she now goes down awake for all her naps and night time sleep and falls asleep on her own. Thank you!!!

She sometimes cries for about 15 minutes but usually no longer than that. I think the two key elements that your system taught me was the importance of the afternoon nap and the falling asleep on her own. She wasn't really having an afternoon nap and she now has between one and a half and two hours and that seems to have made a lot of difference to her. Ditching the dummy was also the best thing I ever did and she no longer wakes me to put it back in during the night. I was getting up between 15 and 20 times a night and now she sleeps through from 7pm to 6am or sometimes even 7am!

I stuck to the routine from The Baby Sleep System and never faltered and now I rarely need to go back in once I have put her down, it is as if she understands that I am not going anywhere, she is not on her own and that bedtime is a good time!"

8   How to Handle Specific Sleep Issues

Now that you have put together and are following your routine, and have a toolkit of strategies to choose from to help your child to learn to sleep, you need to establish which particular sleep problem your child has. The following section covers the most common problems and gives ideas on the appropriate action to take.

8.1   Inappropriate Sleep Associations and Accidental Parenting

The following problems all fall under the general heading of inappropriate sleep associations. In other words, your baby or child cannot get to sleep unless a specific condition or conditions are met.

8.1.1 Your Baby Will Only Fall Asleep While Feeding

This problem is extremely common especially for breast fed babies. When you think about it, it is hardly surprising. The baby feels lovely and snug and warm. He can smell the gorgeous scent of his mother and a little suck every now and again fills his mouth with some delicious milk.

That said it can be completely exhausting for the mum in question. A baby dangling from your boob for 24 hours a day is not everybody's idea of a good time. He can still enjoy his feeds and snuggles, but when he gets in his cot, he needs to be able to fall asleep on his own.

Make the cot as comfortable and welcoming as possible. Install a bright and cheerful musical mobile that plays a jolly song. Wrap a new baby in a swaddle blanket and from 3 months purchase a baby sleeping bag (you should also buy a room thermometer so that you can make sure that you have bought the correct tog rating). Buy your child a lovely soft comforter that he can snuggle and grip.

Start your routine that you have devised. Remember it needs to be appropriate for his age group and your family life. A major part of this routine should be the night-time ritual of bath, feed, book, bed. Put the baby into his cot awake, activate his mobile and begin your selected behaviour management strategy. Be prepared to persevere. Your child has to unlearn and relearn and it will take several nights.

8.1.2 Your Child Needs a Dummy to Get to Sleep

Dummies are of course a form of pacifier. Pacifiers have been used for centuries to calm crying babies and toddlers. Many parents use pacifiers to comfort their children. The Avon Longitudinal Study of Parents and Children (ALSPAC) also known as 'Children of the 90s', reported that two thirds of the mothers in their sample of 10,950 had used a dummy at some point. There is an ongoing debate amongst parents and health professionals about the pros and cons of dummy use and much of this debate is often uninformed.

The most recent scientific evidence suggests that using dummies for babies up to 3 months old can be very beneficial.

- Dummies help very small babies to settle off to sleep.
- Sucking on a pacifier releases chemicals in the brain that can sooth pain, thereby making it useful for babies suffering from colic.

- Premature babies are often given a dummy because it helps them transfer more quickly from tube to bottle feeding by developing the sucking action.

- A report published in the British Medical Journal in December 2005 suggested that dummy use actually protects against SIDS (Sudden Infant Death Syndrome / Cot Death). The reasons why are not fully understood, but it could be because the sucking action helps the baby to control his upper airway or the bulky handle helps to keep the covers away from the baby's face.

The above are not reasons to give every child a dummy, but they can help certain parents and babies in certain circumstances. My advice would be to use a dummy only for the first three months and at bedtime only. At three months transfer the baby into a sleeping bag and take the dummy away. This will reduce the likelihood that the baby will become reliant on it to get to sleep.

The new routine that you are about to introduce should mean that your child is busy doing something for large parts of the day and so it should be possible to distract her from asking for the dummy.

The quickest and least stressful way of stopping dummy use in young children is to simply remove the dummy and bin it. If your child is over the age of two there are a number of strategies that you can use and I have included these in a free e-book available to download at www.babysleepanswers.co.uk.

8.2   Managing Early Waking

Some children are genetically pre-disposed to be early birds. However, this only applies to around 10% to 15% and often they have a parent who needs only six hours sleep themselves.

Most early rising children are up with the larks for other reasons. The children in this category can be helped to sleep in later.

8.2.1   General Reasons for Early Waking

It could well be that your child has had enough sleep. Look at the chart (section 2.3) and add the daytime sleep to the night time sleep that your child takes in a 24 hour period.

A seven month old baby that had a one hour nap in the morning and a two hour nap in the afternoon has used up three hours of his $13\frac{3}{4}$ hours. If he then goes to bed at 7:00pm he should wake at 5:00am! The naps are therefore too frequent, too long or the bedtime hour is too early. The solution lies in dropping naps, reducing naps or putting the child to bed later.

What follows are suggestions for reducing early waking in different aged children.

8.2.2 Newborns

New babies are going to wake several times in the night, including the early morning. However, from the very beginning you do need to start establishing the patterns that you would like to see later. Therefore:

- Develop good sleep habits – introduce a consistent bedtime and nap routine and put the baby down awake in his cot. At this stage be led by your baby. If they are tired put them down for a sleep. A pattern will soon start to emerge.

- Put something in the cot to act as a comforter if they do wake e.g. a blanket or soft toy.

- Help your baby to distinguish between night and day. Administer night feeds in subdued light and fit blackouts to the window.

- Plan the time and length of daytime naps using the sleep time guidelines and wake him if he sleeps longer.

- Do not jump out of bed at the slightest whimper in the early morning. Leave it for a few minutes and see if he settles himself.

- Get your baby up between 6:00am and 8:00am even if you have had a bad night. This consistency will pay off in the long run.

8.2.3 Older Babies

All of the above plus:

- Establish a specific bedtime and consistently timed naps. Bedtime should be between 7:00pm and 8:30pm for this age group. You should be aiming for a nap mid-morning and a nap in the afternoon (not finishing later than 4:30pm). The bedtime routine should be packed with sleep cues as discussed earlier.

- Continue to put the baby down in his cot awake.

- If he cries before 6:00am go into the room, leave the light off and reassure him with your voice or a pat, but do not pick him up. Leave an increasing length of time between the checks – write the checking times down on a piece of paper and then tick them off as you do them. Father can often be the best person to tackle early waking if the mum is the main carer during the day or vice versa.

- Even if the baby has fallen asleep again, get him up at the same regular time. This routine may be hard to start with, but will pay off in the long term.

8.2.4 Toddlers

All of the strategies outlined for babies still apply. However, you can begin to add some extra strategies:

- Reduce naps; many children over 12 months only need one afternoon nap. Drop the morning sleep and move the afternoon nap to an earlier time. Shorten this nap to one and a half hours or less.

- Make sure that the child gets plenty of exercise after the nap so they are tired in the evening.

- Watch the clock until the child starts to look sleepy. Make that her regular bedtime. This can be extended to 9:00pm for the very worst offenders.

- Make it clear to your toddler that they are not to get out of bed. Put a gate across the bedroom door. Tell him you are happy to leave the gate open if he doesn't get out of bed.

8.2.5 Pre-schoolers

All of the strategies outlined so far still apply. However, your child is now at the stage where he can start to take some responsibility for actions and can start to manage his own behaviour. Here are some suggestions on how to encourage this.

- Establish a clear rule "you cannot get out of bed until we tell you".

- Set a lamp on the bedside table which is easy to switch on and off. Tell him he can switch it on so he can see, but he is not to get out of bed.

- Offer choices of what he would like to do if he wakes early e.g. have some books to look at or have a favourite toy at the side of the bed. Offer choices that you are happy to comply with. If you leave it open you might end up with a bed full of play dough! Make sure the toys are safe and not noisy.

- Praise your child when she stays in her bed and doesn't wake anyone else up. Use a reward chart. If she gets out, return her firmly for as many times as it takes.

- Set a clock radio or a toy specially developed for early waking children to a time that you consider to be appropriate. Reward your child for not getting up before the radio comes on, frog pops open etc.

- If the child has a chronic problem start by setting the clock at 5:15am and then moving it forward every 15 minutes, every 3 days.

- Finally, if you are at the end of your tether and have tried everything else, do the unthinkable – set the Sky or Freeview box to CBeebies or leave a DVD in the machine and show her how to switch the television on – guaranteed extra sleep for you! Of course you need to be confident that your child is old enough and that the house is absolutely safe enough for your child to be wandering around it.

8.2.6   Definite No-No's

Some things you should not do:

- Do not let them come into bed with you. This is a bad habit that you do not want to encourage.

- Do not leave toys in a cot for a baby to play with – the game will become "throw the toys out of the cot and scream for someone to come and get them" or they might just use them to climb out, as my eldest son once did.

Be reassured that as the child gets older they will be less inclined to get up early. Think of a typical teenager!

Case Study: Hilary and Isobel

Hilary and her 20 week old daughter Isobel live in Ilkley, West Yorkshire. Hilary started sleep training Isobel using The Baby Sleep System when she was 20 weeks old.

Isobel had been a fractious baby from the off and in the first six weeks had cried for the majority of the day. On top of this she was waking at 4:00am and refusing to go back to sleep for up to three hours. By the time Hilary purchased The Baby Sleep System she was exhausted and desperate.

The Strategy

After corresponding with Hilary through the Baby Sleep Answers forum we worked out what Isobel's key issues were. She had nearly doubled in weight since birth, was healthy and had an excellent day time routine. We quickly established that her day time napping was a little erratic and that she had become very reliant on her dummy to get herself to sleep. As Hilary put it:

"If she spits it out she will cry and I go in the room to replace it - this may happen up to three or four times."

I suggested to Hilary that the first course of action was to stop Isobel's reliance on her dummy.

We also agreed that the naps needed to be more structured in terms of timing and length. I gave Hilary a new routine and advised on how best to implement the improvements.

The Result

After two weeks of hard work Isobel was sleeping through the night on a regular basis. Hilary continued to visit the forum for ongoing support as Isobel went through her developmental stages (i.e. weaning). One of her later posts read:

"Well, everything since we last spoke is going brilliantly. Isobel is now sleeping through the night from her dream feed around 11:00ish until 6:30 - 7:00ish each morning which is fantastic. Dummies are a thing of the past and Isobel just seems so much happier, so thanks for all your help."

9   Siblings and the Baby Sleep System

This is an issue which has been sadly neglected in most of the baby sleep related books on the market. It is however, a subject which is raised a lot by families following the Baby Sleep System.

The action that you take will to a large degree depend on the age of other children in the family and the current sleeping arrangements. Here are a few suggestions that might work for your family:

1. If your children currently share a room, put the older one in your bed. When he has fallen asleep and you have settled the baby you will then be able to transfer him into his own room.

2. Older siblings who can understand should have the situation explained to them. Make it clear that you are helping their brother or sister and although it might be very upsetting to hear their little baby cry, everyone else will get more sleep as a result.

3. If the baby's night time waking is causing older brothers and sisters to get out of bed and so are making the problem worse, introduce a reward chart. He can earn a star if he stays in bed while you sleep train his brother. At the end of 3 days he can have a little treat as a reward.

4. You may consider sending older brothers and sisters to relatives for a few days. The worst two or three nights will then be over when they return.

Finally, just remember that if done consistently, sleep training on average takes less than a week. Think short term pain for long term gain!

10   Advice for Parents of Multiples

10.1   Don't Panic!

Firstly, on a positive note, congratulations for being the proud parents of multiples! I am sure you get fed up of perfect strangers walking up to you in the street, supermarket etc. and thinking it is perfectly alright to announce at the top of their voices that "you've got your hands full". What on earth do they expect you to say!

I am hoping that you have not bought this book out of sheer desperation. I myself am the mother of twins and got them to sleep through the night at 12 weeks old. Even before this they woke, had a full feed and went straight back to sleep so it was a lot easier than I had expected. I know that this is because I had perfected The Baby Sleep System on my first two children.

The information that has been given already in the book is fully relevant to your situation. In summary:

- Plan a routine using the workbook

- Make sure that you get the babies up at their normal waking hour, feed them at breakfast, lunch and tea time and make sure that they take a full milk feed mid morning, mid afternoon and before bed time. You should not leave a gap of longer than four hours between feeds during the day (three hours if they are under 16 weeks). If they do not wake for milk, wake them up at the appointed hour.

- Get out of the house in the morning. I know this is difficult, but try and turn up somewhere at a feed time and you can often rope someone in to help.
- Play with your multiples during the day when they are awake to tire them out.

In addition, utilise the tips set out below that worked very successfully for me.

10.2   Feeding and Sleeping

10.2.1 Daytime

It is vitally important that you get your babies feeding at the same time, or at least with a manageable gap between them (midwives recommend 20 minutes).

Although I had successfully breast fed my first two children, I struggled to breast feed twins (mainly because they were premature, but also because it can be a bit embarrassing feeding two at the same time as you virtually have to get naked).

For the first 10 weeks I expressed the milk and gave it to them out of bottles. I quickly realised that if you prop them up on cushions, you can feed both at the same time. If you have more than two, then rope in some help where you can or feed two and synchronise the other baby or babies' feeds twenty minutes later.

When my twins got older I employed my older children (then aged 4 and 5) to feed one each. By putting the twins on bean bags, Ben and Caitlin only had to hold the bottles. I made sure I stayed close, but at least I could prepare the dinner. By feeding your multiples at the same time you are establishing them in the same routine from the start.

The babies will need to take naps in the day, but these need to be carefully orchestrated. Make sure that you put both or all the babies down to sleep awake (actually it's a bit difficult to rock two or more off to sleep in your arms anyway).

If you are following the advice, for some of the day you will be out of the house. Do not worry if they nap. However, at least one nap per day should be at home and they should be put in their cots at the same time and awake. If you are co-bedding there is no evidence that one will wake the other before they are about nine months old.

10.2.2 Night Time

The same synchronisation rule applies. Feed them at the same time, either by employing your partner or laying them on cushions or in low chairs and feeding them simultaneously. Even if you are managing to breast feed, halve the time it takes by feeding them at the same time.

At night we used to start feeding the twins at around 7:00pm. Being premature they took a long time to take the big pre-night time feed as recommended in the sleep routine. I used to go to bed at 9:30pm and my husband would do a final feed at around 11:30pm. This meant that they were full enough to sleep through until around 3:30am or 4:00am. I then got up when I heard the first twin whimper, woke the other one and fed them only using the landing light. This was to teach them the difference between night and day.

As soon as they had finished their bottles (and I patiently waited for them to take the full feed) I changed their nappies (in the same subdued lighting), swaddled them and put them in their cots awake. The mobile was activated and I quickly and quietly left the room. At 7:00am I woke them again if they didn't wake naturally and repeated the whole routine.

Over the next few weeks I never woke them for a feed in the night, but continued to do so during the day. If one woke for food, I woke the other one. Gradually the length of time between the last feed at 11:30pm and the next one extended. After 10 weeks they could sleep from 11:30pm to 7:00am. Over the next two weeks we brought the evening feed forwards from 11:30pm to 11:00pm and so on, until they were going to bed (with a solid bedtime routine and being put down awake) at 7:30pm.

I am not an exceptional person or mother, but I have stuck rigidly to my own Baby Sleep System and have proved that it works. There are now scores of parents with twins and higher order multiples that have got the same results by following the same advice.

Case Study: Gérald, Elisa and Natalie

Gérald and his partner, live in Southampton with their twin daughters Elisa and Natalie. At 16 months old the family started The Baby Sleep System. They had not had a full night's sleep since the girls were born. Each woke at least twice in the night demanding milk and they screamed until they got it. Gérald's partner was only getting 5 hours sleep in total and only for one or two hours at a stretch.

The couple had tried a variety of different ways to make the twins sleep through the night but although it may have worked for one of them for a little while, it never worked for them both at the same time.

The Strategy

Mum and dad re-evaluated the typical day in the lives of the twins. Using The Baby Sleep System's workbook they introduced a structure which co-ordinated the activities of both girls so that they did most things at the same time. The bedtime routine was revised so that it was the same every night and contained a lot of "sleep cues". As the girls were toddlers rather than babies mum and dad explained that from now on they must get in their beds at bedtime and would be expected to stay there and sleep all night. When they got out of bed they were returned immediately and aside from basic reassurance, night time contact was kept to a minimum.

The Result

As Gérald explains:

"The first couple of nights were quite difficult but after a further five nights, Elisa and Natalie were only waking once or twice and for a few minutes only. Now, we are able to sleep well every night, so a big thank you for that Wendy."

11   Top Tips for a Good Night's Sleep

The points set out below are a summary of the whole book. The reasons why your child has problems getting to sleep or staying asleep are generally straight forward. Check here to make sure that you are doing the things that will help your child to get to sleep, avoiding the things that will hinder.

Do:

1. Establish a proper nap and bedtime routine so that your child is taking sleep in the right places.

2. Try and keep noise to a minimum for the 15 minutes after your baby has gone to bed. This will help him to drift gently off to sleep.

3. Let your baby learn to fall asleep on his own in his cot.

4. Try and wean your baby off a dummy once he reaches three months old. It can lead to difficulties if the baby is associating it with going to sleep and it then falls out in the night.

5. Use a room thermometer and a sleeping bag to ensure that your baby does not get too hot or too cold. The sleeping bag should come with instructions about room temperature and appropriate tog values.

6. Make sure that if old enough your child is aware of the boundaries for bedtime behaviour. Stick to them yourself i.e. do not give in to "just 5 more minutes" or "I need another drink".

Do Not:

1. Use the bedroom as a place of punishment. It should always be a pleasant place to go.

2. Go to your baby immediately if he whimpers or calls out in the night. He may well settle himself back to sleep.

3. Allow any children older than nine months a nap that finishes later than 4:30pm. This will make it harder to go to sleep at night.

4. Give your baby or child high sugar treats or soft drinks with caffeine within two hours of going to bed.

5. Feed or rock your baby to sleep. Put him down awake.

6. Once the bedtime routine begins don't go back into the living areas of the house. Go directly from the bathroom to the bedroom.

7. Do not engage in anything that will stimulate your child for an hour before bed e.g. TV, rowdy games. Do something together quietly like read a book or do a simple puzzle.

8. Put your baby to bed hungry. Make sure that he has had enough milk and solid food if appropriate.

12 Extra Support

12.1 Online Support Forum

Getting a baby to sleep through the night can be a very difficult and emotional experience. That is why I would not leave you to do it on your own. The Baby Sleep Answers website (www.babysleepanswers.co.uk) has an online forum that is open, exclusively, to all purchasers of The Baby Sleep System. The Forum is free to purchasers of the book and you can post questions 24 hours a day, 7 days a week.

Users are supported by the "Dream Team" a group of volunteers who advise parents who post on the forum. They have all:

- Experienced a range of problems and used the forum to best effect.
- Understand the most popular techniques and have used at least one.
- Have babies that now sleep through.

The team are very keen to support new members on the forum and logon regularly.

Posting a message is easy.

1. Go to www.babysleepanswers.co.uk and click on the Online Support Forum link on the home page.

2. Type in the username and password which is printed on the back inside cover of this book. Click on **Login**. Further information about how to use the Forum is displayed once you have logged in.

12.2   Exclusive Individual One to One Support

Additional support is available from a fully trained sleep councillor via the Forum, for a fee. The Councillor will ask you to complete a comprehensive questionnaire detailing your child's specific problems and they will then provide you with a step by step plan. The Councillor will continue to support you for a period of 30 days via a private online thread.

12.3   Baby Sleep Answers Website

The Baby Sleep Answers website supports the Baby Sleep System and is updated regularly with the latest sleep related news and articles. Check the website regularly while you are implementing the programme.

12.4   Health Visitor

The role of your health visitor is to:

- Listen, advise and support people from all backgrounds and age groups.

- Deliver child health programmes and run parenting groups.

- Work in partnership with your family to develop and agree tailored health plans addressing individual parenting and health needs, this includes baby sleep problems.

- Offer counselling to people on issues such as post natal depression.

Your health visitor is there to support you. If you have any worries or concerns use her as a resource and do not be embarrassed about discussing worries and fears with her. The chances are that she has heard it all before and she certainly will not judge you or tell you that you are inadequate.

12.5   Feedback

Six weeks after you have started The Baby Sleep System you will receive an email inviting you to complete our online feedback form. I would love to hear from you even if you have had difficulties. I am continually improving the system and it is the feedback I receive from parents that helps make it better.

Finally, if you have found this book useful then please recommend us to a friend.

Good luck

Wendy Dean

The
Baby Sleep System
Workbook

Child's Name:	
Date of Birth:	
Date System Started:	

About the Workbook

This workbook is a key feature of The Baby Sleep System. It allows you to fully understand your child's non-sleeping behaviour and address this with practical action. You can use it on a daily basis to plan your routine and to plot your progress.

Completing The Routine Planner

You can complete this as you work your way through the book. You should start by putting in the feed times. These are calculated from the time your baby wakes up. The interval between each feed will depend on the age of your baby (see section 3). Naps can then be interspersed as appropriate for the age of your child (see section 5). In addition the Routine Planner enables you to plot your dream feed and the methods that you will be using at key points through a 24 hour period to help your child nap and settle at night. Finally you can plan your activities for the week.

   At first you will need to tweak your routine over several days until you have a plan for the week that becomes the norm.

The Routine Planner

Here is an example of a completed planner designed for a six month old baby:

Time	Wake up	Milk Feed	Solid Meal	Activity	Nap	Tank	Bed-time Routine	Dream Feed	Night Feed Approach	Behaviour Management Technique
06:00	X	X								
06:30			X							
09:30					X					PUPDCD
10:00		X		Coffee morning						
12:00			X							
12:30					X					PUPDCD
14:30		X								
17:00			X							
18:30		X					X			CC
22:30								X		
03:00									Calorie maximisation approach	CC
07:00	X	X								

Here is blank Routine Planner for you to complete. You may need to create a different one for each day to begin with. Permission is granted to photocopy this page for personal use. Copies can also be downloaded from the Baby Sleep Answers website.

Time	Wake up	Milk Feed	Solid Meal	Activity	Nap	Tank	Bed-time Routine	Dream Feed	Night Feed Approach	Behaviour Management Technique

Monitoring Baby's Sleep Patterns

This section of the workbook will enable you to track your child's sleep patterns. The 24 hour day has been divided up into two hour slots. You need to record how many minutes your child spent in that two hour slot sleeping, feeding or doing an activity. The total number of hours spent sleeping will probably not change. What you are aiming to do is to increase the amount of sleep that is being taken between 6:00pm and 6:00am.

Once again, permission is granted to photocopy these sheets for personal use. Copies can also be downloaded from the Baby Sleep Answers website.

The Baby Sleep System

Day: _____

	Sleep	Feeding	Activity or Playing
06:00-08:00			
08:00-10:00			
10:00-12:00			
12:00-14:00			
14:00-16:00			
16:00-18:00			
18:00-20:00			
20:00-22:00			
22:00-00:00			
00:00-02:00			
02:00-04:00			
04:00-06:00			
TOTAL			

Day: _____

	Sleep	Feeding	Activity or Playing
06:00-08:00			
08:00-10:00			
10:00-12:00			
12:00-14:00			
14:00-16:00			
16:00-18:00			
18:00-20:00			
20:00-22:00			
22:00-00:00			
00:00-02:00			
02:00-04:00			
04:00-06:00			
TOTAL			

babysleepanswers.co.uk

Further Reading

Healthy Sleep Habits, Happy Child: A Step-by-step Programme for a Good Night's Sleep (Paperback)
by Marc Weissbluth

Help Your Baby to Sleep
by Penny Hames

No-Cry Sleep Solution for Toddlers and Preschoolers
by Elizabeth Pantley

Sleeping Through the Night: How Infants, Toddlers, and Their Parents Can Get a Good Night's Sleep
by Jodi A. Mitchell

Solve Your Child's Sleep Problems: A Practical and Comprehensive Guide for Parents
by Richard Ferber

Solving Children's Sleep Problems: A Step-by-step Guide for Parents
by Lyn Quine

Teach Your Child to Sleep: Solving Sleep Problems from Newborn Through Childhood
by Millpond Sleep Clinic

The Baby Whisperer Solves All Your Problems
by Tracy Hogg with Melinda Blau

The No-cry Sleep Solution: Gentle Ways to Help Your Baby Sleep Through the Night
by Elizabeth Pantley

The Sleep Book for Tired Parents: Help for Solving Children's Sleep Problems
by Rebecca Huntley, Kathleen Kerr (Illustrator)

Useful Contacts

Cry-sis

Cry-sis offers support for families with excessively crying, sleepless and demanding babies. You can contact the Cry-sis helpline on 08451 228 669

(08451 ACT NOW) 7 days a week 9am-10pm (GMT). The answering service will give you the phone number of volunteer contacts, who once had similar problems.

Website: www.cry-sis.org.uk

The Foundation for the Study of Infant Deaths (FSID)

The Foundation for the Study of Infant Deaths (FSID) is the UK's leading baby charity working to prevent sudden deaths and promote health. FSID funds research, supports bereaved families and promotes safe baby care advice.

FSID Helpline: 020 7233 2090
               9am to 11pm, Monday to Friday
               6-11pm on weekends and Bank Holidays

Website: www.fsid.org.uk

MAMA – The Meet a Mum Association

The Meet A Mum Association was created to try and help thousands of mothers who feel depressed and isolated when their babies are born.

Website: www.mama.co.uk

The National Childbirth Trust

Alexandra House
Oldham Terrace
Acton
London   W3 6NH
Tel: 0870 770 3236
Textphone: 020 8993 6714

Enquiries Line: 0870 444 8707
(9am to 5pm, Monday to Thursday; 9am to 4pm on Friday)

Membership Line:
08709 908040 (9am to 5pm, Monday to Friday)

Breastfeeding Line:
0870 444 8708 (8am to 10pm, seven days a week)

Pregnancy and Birth Line:
0870 444 8709 (11am to 2pm, Monday to Friday)
Fax: 0870 770 3237

Email: enquiries@nct.org.uk

Twins and Multiple Births Association (TAMBA)

2 The Willows
Gardner Road
Guildford
GU1 4PG
Tel: 0870 770 3305

If you would like advice or support about your multiples, please call Twinline where you can speak to another parent of twins or more.

Twinline: 0800 138 0509

Website: www.tamba.org.uk